What You'll See From Where I Stand

A Panoramic View of the Bible Including the Time Between the Testaments

by Brenda Poinsett

Copyright Brenda Poinsett, 2018
All Rights Reserved
Printed in the United States of America
By Create Space

Under International Copyright Law, no part of this publication may be reproduced, stored, or transmitted by any means—electronic, mechanical, photographic (photocopy), recording, or otherwise—without written permission from the author.

ISBN-13: 978-1720323990

Contents

Introduction: Where You Stand Makes a Difference in What You See

Part I The Old

1 God Created, Choice Separated	7
2 Light Needed, People Called	9
3 Call Answered, Faith Tested	11
4 Test Passed, Faith Endures	13
5 Famine Threatened, People Saved	15
6 Freedom Granted, Law Given	17
7 Land Settled, People Unsettled	19
8 King Wanted, Kingdom Comes	21
9 Kingdom Splits, Prophets Warn	23
10 Exile Solidified, Knowledge Gained	25
11 Remnant Returned, Rebuilding Needed	27

Part II The Time In Between

12 Talk Expanded, Lifestyle Challenged	30
13 Conformity Demanded, Courage Responded	32
14 Freedom Gained, Freedom Lost	34
15 Prophets Quiet, Rules Prevail	36

Part III The New

16 Light Arrives, People Unaware	38
17 Darkness Hovers, Light Shines	40
18 Power Comes, Light Spreads	42
19 Questions Asked, Answers Given	44
20 Troubles Threaten, Light Endures	46

Bibliography

Acknowledgements

Introduction

Where You Stand Makes a Difference
in What You See

A man I know resides in a valley below a high mountain range. He lives a very stressful life, but Alan says, "When I go up into the mountains, my stress fades away." As he looks out over the valley where he lives and works, everything looks different. While he still has problems, his view changes. The problems no longer seem so formidable.

Lou, a friend of mine, prefers to sit near the front when she attends church. She said, "When I sit in the back I notice too much! People whispering. Teenagers texting. Children punching each other. Old men sleeping. When I move to the front, the distractions are eliminated. I can better see God."

Where we stand—or sit!—makes a difference in what we see. For a long time, I looked for a place to stand where I could better see the Bible. It wasn't that I didn't read the Bible. I did but its many bits and pieces didn't seem to fit together.

In high school, I asked my Sunday school teachers questions like these, Did the prophecies of the Old Testament prophets come true? Where did the synagogues come from? They are not in the Old Testament, but they are in the New. Why did David and Solomon not go to church but Peter and Paul did? I kept thinking, *Surely there is some kind of connection that holds the contents together.*

In college, I still couldn't get a grip on the Bible's contents. I read my Bible daily and participated in Bible studies, but always with a sense of uneasiness. I kept thinking there had to be something more going on, something bigger than I can see.

And then in seminary, I stood in a place where I could see the Bible as a whole. I was taking a class in biblical backgrounds. The class met in a large lecture hall with elevated flooring. If you entered the room from the back, you were at its highest point. The lectern and chalkboards were down in front, at the room's lowest point.

One day, when I entered the room at the back, I saw the professor had put an outline on the chalkboard. Actually he used several chalkboards. As I starting walking down toward the front, I started reading. I stopped when I realized it was an outline of the Bible's contents. As my eyes scanned the outline, I said to myself, *Why it does all fit! The parts do fit together!*

I enthusiastically took notes that day, getting the whole outline on paper. As I studied the outline, I felt like I had been handed the missing pieces of a puzzle. The Bible started making more sense. My uneasiness faded.

From then on, even though I had much to learn about the Bible—and still do—I felt like I had a grip on its contents. I could see how the main events and big ideas of the Bible connected. The Bible became a much richer and more understandable book.

Because the outline was such a breakthrough for me, I shared it with others, particularly with my students at Oakland City University's Bedford (Indiana) campus. I quickly learned that a narrative worked better for sharing than an outline. Most of us respond better to stories than we do to outlines. It's this narrative that I want to share in this book.

I call it a panoramic view because it takes a broad sweeping look at the whole Bible. While it is broad, covering hundreds of years, the view is also short so it can be grasped in one reading. This facilitates seeing the Bible as a whole.

A short view means a lot of details must be left out. Your favorite Bible story may not be included. The outline may seem oversimplified at times. That's because it is! I don't want anyone to get bogged down with details or particular passages and quit reading. I want the full view to be grasped.

Rest assured, though, that we will highlight and connect the significant events of the Bible. We'll place them in order of their occurrence to reveal the Bible's complete story allowing us to see how God works in broad strokes.

I've also included in this narrative what happened in the time between the Old Testament and the New Testament. Learning what occurred in those in-between years answered many of the questions I had about the Bible. For example, now I know the origin of the synagogues!

I offer this panorama as a tool for reading and studying the Bible—not for developing doctrine or a system of beliefs. My purpose is not to change anyone's mind or persuade them to believe the way I believe. My motive is to help people have a better comprehension of the Bible to facilitate their reading and understanding.

How about you? Are you like I was, needing a grip on the contents of the Bible? If you do, then "stand with me." Together let's take a wide, sweeping look, one that covers the Bible from beginning to end including the time between the testaments. This look will heighten your understanding of the Bible, increase your knowledge, and provide you a framework that you build on as you continue to read and to study the Bible. This panoramic view will enrich your Bible study and give you a historical perspective. You'll see that the Bible is a story of love, of a chosen people, of a land, of a Savior, of a new people, and of hope for the future. Who knows? You may even see yourself as you never have before because where you stand makes a difference in what you see.

The Old Testament

Chapter 1

God Created, Choice Separated

The Bible opens with these words, "In the beginning God created the heavens and the earth" (Genesis 1:1 KJV). The earth was formless and desolate; everything was engulfed in darkness. The first thing God did was to speak light into existence. He said, "Let there be light: and there was light" (Genesis 1:1 KJV).

He went on day by day to create a wonderful world and creatures to occupy it. The last of those creatures was man and woman, Adam and Eve. "God blessed them" (Genesis 1:27a KJV) in many ways.

He gave them a place to live and to thrive—a lush garden that included trees, fresh water rivers, and good things to eat. In this environment, all their physical and material needs were supplied.

God gave them meaningful work to perform. They were to till and keep the garden. They were to be fruitful and to multiply.

He created man and woman in His likeness. This doesn't mean He created little gods. Rather it means He created humans so interaction would be possible. Like God, they could talk, laugh, remember, feel and think. More importantly, they could love and connect so they could enjoy a meaningful relationship with Him, and they did. God walked with Adam and Eve in the garden and had conversations with them.

God gave them a choice, indicating He didn't want forced or mechanical love. He said, "You are free to eat from any tree in the garden; but you must not eat of the tree of knowledge of good and evil" (Genesis 2:16b-17a NIV). God desired authentic love and interaction so He didn't create puppets or robots, creatures who couldn't think and who acted automatically. Instead, God created people who could genuinely respond to Him and interact with Him.

How did Adam and Eve respond? They did what they wanted instead of what God wanted. They chose to eat the fruit God told them not to eat. When they did, they no longer felt comfortable in His presence. They hid from Him. Going contrary to God's will has this effect. It makes us feel separated from Him. It is as if a chasm develops between us. God is on one side and men and women are on the other side.

In addition to feeling estranged from God as a result of their choice, man and woman had to leave the garden. Now instead of having all their needs met, they had to work hard and endure pain and suffering. While they could no longer till and keep the garden, they could, though, still multiply and fill up the earth, and they did.

From Adam and Eve onward, as humans increased, filling up the earth, men and women chose to do what they wanted instead of what God wanted. Jealousy. Murder. Drunkenness. Pride. Selfishness. Wickedness. Corruption. Violence. The gap between men and women and God intensified. Individuals, families and groups couldn't seem to grasp that God loved them. They couldn't see that He wanted to share Himself, His goodness and His work with them. That gap between them seemed shrouded in darkness for it was now hard for men and women to see God, let alone connect with Him.

What's God going to do about this dilemma? After all, it was His idea to create the world and its inhabitants. This wasn't some plan that a person came up with and asked God to do. God was the *Initiator*. He's the One who desired interaction. What's He going to do about the gap between Him and men and women? Will He leave things as they are with His being on one side and people on the other? Or will He do something to span the gap and break through the darkness? What's going to happen?

Chapter 2
Light Needed, People Called

God never stopped wanting to share Himself, His love, His goodness and His work with men and women. The people—the ones now scattered through out the earth—were mostly oblivious to this possibility. The darkness that surrounded the gap between them and God interfered with their seeing Him. God, though, continued in His desire to share Himself so He called a particular people to be a light to shine through the darkness. How this group of people lived would let men, women, boys and girls see God and be drawn to Him.

This doesn't mean that God looked down to earth, spotted a group of people that was holy as He is holy, and gave them the task of representing Him. God chose people who were mostly unaware of Him and who weren't thinking in terms of pleasing God let alone representing Him. Consequently, they needed help in becoming a distinctive people who would reveal God to others. To develop as God's representatives, they needed help. They needed a leader, a land, and eventually, laws.

God called Abraham (first known as Abram) to be their leader. Abraham was probably caught off guard by God's call. It wasn't like he had been contemplating serving God or even that he had any special awareness of Him. He wasn't expecting a major life change. Abraham was living in Heron (probably a place in Turkey) as part of a large family. He was married to Sarah (first known as Sarai) and looking after his aged father. He didn't seek God out and ask Him to give him a role. No, it was the other way around. God sought out Abraham. The *Initiator* interrupted Abraham's life so His will could be accomplished.

God said to Abraham, "Leave your country, your people and your father's household and go to a land I will show you. I will make you into a great nation and I will bless you; I will make your name great, and you will be a blessing. *I will bless those who bless you, and whoever curses you I will curse; and all peoples on earth will be blessed through you*" (Genesis 12:1b-3 NIV, author's italics).

Abraham's initial reaction surely must have been "You've got to be kidding!" God, whom he couldn't see or touch, was asking him to leave his people, to leave what was familiar, and go to another country! At age seventy-five, Abraham wasn't interested in starting over in some unknown land. Besides, he probably didn't want to leave his extended family. Ancient families had strong ties. They stayed together.

There was, however, some enticement in the call. If Abraham were to go, God promised him that several things would occur.

- "I will make of you a great nation" which included having many descendants.
- "I will bless you."
- "I will make your name great."
- "You will be a blessing."

Implied in this call is the idea that Abraham's family would gain a homeland. Why would God do this? He chose Abraham and his descendants so that "all peoples on earth" would "be blessed" (Genesis 12:3 NIV). This doesn't mean they were God's favorites; rather they were chosen for responsibility so that "all families of the earth" would be blessed (Genesis 12:3).

The special responsibility of Abraham's descendants was to communicate God, His love, and His goodness to the world. How they acted, how they reflected God, would draw people to Him. If Abraham's descendants didn't reveal God, other nations wouldn't learn about Him.

Whether this representation became reality hinged on Abraham's response to God's call. Would Abraham leave his home, his extended family, and his familiar surroundings to go to a foreign land? Would he accept this challenging adventure? Did Abraham believe enough in a God he could not see to leave his home and go to a new country? Would the Chosen People become a light to shine across the gulf of separation and draw men and women to God?

Chapter 3

Call Answered, Faith Tested

Sometimes you have to get away from all that is familiar in order to fully realize who you are. If Abraham and his descendants were to fully be God's representatives, they needed a place to develop their distinctiveness. They needed a place where they could be molded as a group. Whether Abraham realized this or not, he "put his trust in the Lord" (Genesis 15:6a TEV) and set out for the Promised Land.

Going was a test of faith since he didn't know what he would encounter. He knew nothing about the people already living there. Would they be welcoming or antagonistic? Neither did he know what the terrain of the land would be. The decision to go, to follow God's instructions, certainly stretched his faith and increased Abraham's sensitivity to hearing God speak.

When Abraham left Haran, he took Sarah, his nephew Lot, their accumulated possessions and their workers, and set out for the Promised Land. The land was Canaan, located in the area of the world where Israel is today.

Once there, Abraham, Sarah, Lot, and their workers moved from place to place in and among the Canaanites. They continually looked for water and grazing land for their flocks. They also looked for confirmation that this was indeed the land God had in mind for them. It was tempting to doubt with so many people already living in Canaan. *Are we in the right place? Is there room here for us?*

From time to time, God reassured Abraham there was room, and that there would be room. He would bless and prosper him. At the same time, God had expectations of Abraham and the Chosen People. They were to be a loyal and faithful people, distinguishable from the other groups around them. This included having a physical mark: all males were to be circumcised, something other nations did not practice.

As Abraham claimed God's land promise, he wondered about the many descendants God had promised. He and Sarah hadn't even had one child. They were getting older and older, and yet no heir was forthcoming. How could there be *many* descendants when there wasn't even *one*? Was God keeping some of His promises but not all of them? Or did this mean God was growing him by testing his faith? If He was, how was Abraham going to react?

When Abraham was a hundred years old and Sarah was ninety, Isaac was born! His faithfulness was rewarded. Many descendants were now possible. In their happiness, Abraham didn't know that a greater faith test was still to come.

When Isaac was older, God commanded Abraham to sacrifice him. He said, "Take your only son, Isaac, whom you love so much, and go to the land of Moriah. There on a mountain that I will show you, offer him as a sacrifice to me" (Genesis 22:2 TEV).

What?! Hard to believe that God who loves would ask a parent to sacrifice a child, isn't it? The very thought is horrifying. And as if that isn't awful enough, the death of Isaac would undo the promise that Abraham would be the father of a great nation. His death would negate the possibility of Abraham's descendants being God's light to the other nations.

Abraham must have beat his chest in grief and agonized in his soul as he faced this crucial test. Perhaps he wondered, Should I have stayed in my ancestral home? Should I have stayed with my family? Why did I think following a God I can't see or touch was the right thing to do? Abraham had faced many faith challenges in establishing the Chosen People in the Promised Land, but this was the greatest. This was huge. Will Abraham pass this test?

Chapter 4

Test Passed, Faith Endures

Abraham set out to do what God asked him to do: sacrifice his son. He built an altar and arranged wood on it. Abraham tied up Isaac and placed him on top of the wood. Then Abraham picked up a knife to kill Isaac and start the fire that would consume him. "But the angel of the Lord called to him from heaven, 'Abraham, Abraham!' (Genesis 22:11 TEV).

"He answered, 'Yes, here I am'" (Genesis 22:11c TEV).

"'Don't hurt the boy or do anything to him,' [the angel] said. 'Now I know that you have obedient reverence for God, because you have not kept back your only son from me' (Genesis 22:12 TEV).

"Abraham looked around and saw a ram caught in a bush by its horns. He went and got it and offered it as a burnt offering instead of his son" (Genesis 22:13 TEV).

Abraham passed the faith test! He trusted God so much that he was willing to sacrifice his son. This strengthened him as a person and as a leader of God's people. Not only would he be the physical father of many descendants, but he would be a spiritual father as well. He would be the father of the faithful. Would his legacy live on?

Abraham was reassured that it would. God's messenger, the angel of the Lord, said to Abraham, "I promise that I will give you as many descendants as there are stars in the sky or grains of sand along the seashore . . . All the nations will ask me to bless them as I have blessed your descendants—*all because you obeyed my command*" (Genesis 22:17a,18 TEV, author's italics).

After Abraham's death, Isaac carried on his father's legacy even though he wasn't as courageous as Abraham was. When he encountered friction with the Canaanites as he searched for adequate pastures and water for their flocks, he usually chose to move on rather than argue. He was weak in many ways; still, Isaac followed God and led the Chosen People. Later in Isaac's life, God renewed the promise of land he had made to Abraham, and then the same promise was passed on to Isaac's son, Jacob.

Jacob wasn't the peace loving man that his father, Isaac, was. Neither was he a strong person like his grandfather Abraham. Jacob was weak in character, inconsistent in his behavior and an escapist when it came to facing harsh realities. For example, after he cheated his brother, Esau, Jacob wanted to avoid him altogether. When a meeting seemed inevitable, he sent his family on ahead to meet Esau. Jacob spent the night alone. In the darkness, he wrestled with a manifestation of God in the form of a man (some say angel). Here was someone Jacob couldn't escape from. Here was someone he had to face. As he wrestled with the angel, Jacob said to Him, "I will not let you go unless you bless me" (Genesis 32:26b NIV).

God responded by blessing Jacob. To signify this, He gave Jacob a new name. God called him Israel–a name that figures prominently in the story of God's calling and using a people. From this point on, the Chosen People (Jacob's descendants) will be known as Israelites. Jacob fathered twelve sons, and they became heads of tribes known as the Twelve Tribes of Israel. Eventually, a long time in the future, this land–the land promised first to Abraham–will be called Israel.

Now that Jacob is a changed man, will anything change? Will he help God's people develop in the Promised Land? What would happen if they were disconnected from the land? Would it matter? Would it interfere with their being the light God wants them to be?

Chapter 5

Famine Threatened, People Saved

Jacob made a mistake that parents sometimes do; he favored one child over the others. Jacob liked Joseph the best of his twelve sons. His preference was obvious to Joseph's brothers sparking jealousy and resentment. Their feelings were so strong they wanted to kill Joseph. Instead they sold him to traders traveling through Canaan on their way to Egypt.

Once in Egypt, the traders sold Joseph to Potiphar who worked for Pharaoh, the king. Potiphar was the captain of the palace guard. Joseph's work pleased Potiphar. His wife, however, wasn't interested in the quality of Joseph's work. She saw him as a possible lover and tried to seduce him. Joseph, though, would not succumb to her overtures. Angry over being rejected, she lied about Joseph to Potiphar. She said, "That Israelite slave you hired came into my room and tried to rape me." Potiphar was furious and had Joseph put in prison.

Joseph made the best of his imprisonment. He became a warden in the prison and helped the other prisoners. One thing in particular that he did was to interpret their dreams.

Later, when Pharaoh needed help figuring out the meaning of some disturbing dreams, one of the prisoners Joseph had helped–one who was now free–remembered Joseph's ability to interpret dreams. When he mentioned this, Pharaoh sent for Joseph and told him his dreams. Joseph helped Pharaoh understand that a terrible famine was going to occur. He advised the Egyptians to store up grain in preparation for the lean years.

Recognizing the caliber of person Joseph was, Pharaoh asked him to oversee the years of plenty and the years of famine. Joseph directed the Egyptians to store up grain during the plentiful years so they would have food to eat when the famine occurred.

The famine was widespread, affecting Joseph's family back in Canaan. The Israelites, though, weren't aware a famine was coming. They weren't prepared so when Jacob's family heard there was food in Egypt, they traveled there. They got not only food, they got a huge surprise! They saw Joseph, who they never expected to ever see again.

The brothers were terrified. *What would Joseph do to them?* Joseph amazed them. He forgave them. He realized God had been at work in the painful experiences of his life. Joseph said, "God sent me ahead of you to rescue you . . . and to make sure that you and your descendants survive . . . You plotted evil against me, but God turned it into good, in order to preserve the lives of many people . . ." (Genesis 45:5b,7, 50:20 TEV).

The Chosen People are now together again, although they are not in the land God promised them. They survived the famine, but can they survive living outside the Promised Land?

At first, it appeared they could. The Israelites thrived in Egypt and grew exceedingly numerous as they tended their flocks and those of Pharaoh's as well.

The Egyptians treated the Israelites well as long as Joseph was alive. After his death, a Pharaoh who "knew not Joseph" (Exodus 1:8 KJV) grew alarmed at the growing number of Israelites. He was unaware of what Joseph had done for the Egyptians. He was troubled by the growing Israelite community, so he made them slaves. The Israelites were forced to work in fields and on building sites for long hours in dreadful conditions. The Egyptians crushed "their spirits with hard labor" (Exodus 1:11a TEV) and "had no pity on them" (Exodus 1:13-14 TEV).

As their circumstances became more and more unbearable, God's people cried out to God to deliver them from their misery. They had been saved from the perils of a famine; would God now save them from a life of slavery?

Chapter 6

Freedom Granted, Law Given

God heard the cries of His people. He delivered them from the perils of slavery by calling Moses to lead them out of bondage. The Exodus from Egypt wasn't easy to achieve; the Pharaoh didn't want to lose his work force. Through a series of divinely sent plagues, Moses forced Pharaoh to set the Israelites free. With Moses leading, God's people headed towards the Promised Land.

You would think the Israelites would be ecstatic and cooperative as they left Egypt and followed Moses. Instead, they griped and complained along the way. They grumbled about what they had to eat and worried over whether they would have water to drink. It was evident that these people needed guidelines for living. Just because they were "chosen" to reveal God to others didn't mean they were spiritually mature and lived exemplary lives. They needed parameters on how to live, and God provided those as they traveled to the Promised Land.

God started by reminding them of who He was. He said to them, "I am the Lord thy God, which have brought thee out of the land of Egypt, out of the house of bondage" (Exodus 20:2 KJV). He was the reason they were free. And then through Moses, God gave His people instructions for living. He said,

"Thou shalt have no other gods before me.

"Thou shalt not make unto thee any graven image. . .

"Thou shalt not bow down thyself to them, nor serve them . . .

"Thou shalt not take the name of the Lord thy God in vain . . .

"Remember the Sabbath day, to keep it holy . . .

"Honor thy father and thy mother . . .

"Thou shalt not kill.

"Thou shalt not commit adultery.

"Thou shalt not steal.

"Thou shalt not bear false witness . . .

"Thou shalt not covet . . ." (Exodus 20:2-4a, 5a,7a,8,12a,13-16a,17a KJV).

These Ten Commandments, if followed, would help the Israelites connect with God and live peaceably with each other. Their quality of life would improve but more importantly, they would be a distinctive people unlike those who lived around them. This would enable the Chosen People to introduce others to God and reveal His love for them.

In addition to the Ten Commandments, God gave them worship guidelines, including instructions for building a tabernacle—a traveling worship center. The tabernacle's mobility would allow God's people to connect with Him wherever they were. He gave them instructions for establishing priests from the tribe of Levi, for making sacrificial offerings, and for observing feasts and festivals to keep their heritage alive and God's purpose for them in mind. With their cooperation, all of these things would work together to mold them into being a light to draw people to God. But would they cooperate? Would they follow the instructions?

They had a choice to make, and as we have seen, choices come with consequences. If the Chosen People obeyed and kept the laws, they would be blessed. If they didn't, they would experience troubles and difficulties. The people said, "We will do everything that the Lord has said" (Exodus 24:3 TEV).

This would prove to be easier said than done. Right away, the Israelites reneged on their commitment. They ignored the second commandment. They worshipped a god they made—a god they could see—instead of the unseen God of Abraham, Isaac and Jacob. Moses pleaded with God to forgive them, and He did, so surely this breach will be a one time thing. After all, in addition to forgiveness, God has rescued them from slavery. He's given them leaders, laws, and a soon-to-be reclaimed land, won't that be enough to help them worship only God and be the light He wants them to be?

Chapter 7

Land Settled, People Unsettled

As they neared the Promised Land, the Israelites faced the challenge of conquering it. Canaanites and other groups were living there. Reclaiming the Promised Land meant defeating these groups. For this, God's people needed a strong military leader. Joshua was their man!

Before his death, Moses had groomed Joshua for the task of conquering and settling the Promised Land. Joshua was capable, competent and determined. Under his leadership, the land of Canaan would be theirs. All would be well, the people presumed, once the land was conquered, and they were settled.

Joshua led the Israelites into the Promised Land. He directed Israel's armies in destroying the main strong holds so God's people were able to claim the land. Joshua then divided the land, giving each of the twelve tribes—with the exception of Levi—a specific area in which to live. The Levi tribe was to provide the priests and tabernacle workers. They were to be supported by tithes from the other tribes so land space wasn't needed for them.

Unfortunately, the Israelites didn't do a thorough job of conquering the Canaanites, and this became their undoing after Joshua died. As they looked at other groups living among them, they were attracted to their lifestyle and to their ways. For example, the Israelites, who had been herders and shepherds, became farmers in the Promised Land. Their crops didn't do well, and yet they noticed that the crops of their neighbors prospered.

I imagine their thought processes went something like this: *Why are they successful? Why do their crops thrive? Our neighbors worship other gods so perhaps that's the key. If their crops do well, wouldn't ours do well too if we worshiped their gods?*

At any rate, God's people, whom the law, if you remember, instructed not to have any other gods, began worshiping the idols of their neighbors. They didn't abandon worshiping the God of Abraham, Isaac, and Jacob; they simply added the worship of other gods. Evidently, they wanted to cover all bases, but God's covenant relationship with them—the one they had agreed to—had said, "Thou shalt have no other gods."

The Israelites forgot all that God had done for their ancestors and what He had called them to do. This forgetfulness weakened them. As a result, they often found themselves oppressed. When this happened, the Chosen People cried out to God, "Help us." God loved them so much that He mercifully sent them military deliverers called judges to rescue them. Once rescued, they felt safe again. A plateau of peacefulness would follow, but eventually temptation would raise its ugly head again, and they would give in and live like their neighbors. They wouldn't live the way God wanted them to live.

When they were obedient, earnestly trying to please God, they were blessed. When they were disobedient, they experienced trouble in the way of oppression. Miserable and frightened, they cried out to God for a deliverer. God responded each time by sending judges such as Deborah, Gideon and Samson to get them out of trouble. When they did, peace reigned for a while. Peace never lasted, though, because God's people would once again be disobedient. Like Adam and Eve, they chose to do what they wanted instead of what God wanted.

This cycle repeated itself over and over. Consequently, chances for their being the light God wanted them to be appeared dismal. Rather than seeing God as a great God to serve, the Israelites saw Him as their rescuer in times of desperation. Instead of trying to please God, the Israelites did what was right in their own eyes (see Judges 21:25). What would it take to break the cycle? Was it even possible?

Chapter 8

King Wanted, Kingdom Comes

The judges served largely in local crises. They were not leaders who served all twelve tribes so no leader was on the scene to unite the people as Moses and Joshua once had. Rather the tribes existed as a loose federation—related by heritage but without a sense of needing to work together. As the Israelites faced crisis after crisis in the Promised Land, they concluded that having a strong, visible leader might solve their problems. They expressed their desire to Samuel, a judge who was also a priest and a prophet.

"A king, a king, that's what we need," they told Samuel.

Samuel warned them of the consequences they would suffer if they were ruled by an earthly king instead of being ruled by God. Still, they insisted, "We want a king!"

Samuel anointed a young man by the name of Saul to be king. Under Saul's leadership, the tribes begin working together and growing in power. Saul made mistakes in leadership and in his spiritual life, but still he motivated the tribes to start working together. In a way, you could say he launched a United Kingdom.

The unifying and strengthening of God's people continued under the next king, David. Under his rule, the kingdom expanded geographically, religious practices were encouraged, and the people worked together. Part of David's brilliance as a leader was establishing a capital—a permanent place where the people could rally together and function as a body. The capital he established was Jerusalem, a city in the center of the Promised Land. David made Jerusalem the headquarters for their religious life by having the tabernacle, their traveling worship center, brought to the city. Life was now brighter for God's people.

As the nation grew in size and wealth under David's reign, he desired to build God a permanent place of worship, a temple. God said, "No," to David's request. Too much blood was on David's hands through all the conquering he had done to enlarge the nation. The temple needed to be built by a man of peace which was David's son, Solomon.

Solomon was the United Kingdom's third king, and he had the Temple built in Jerusalem. Solomon brought the United Kingdom to its highest point of wealth and splendor. Unified and focused, it looked as if circumstances were ripe for God's people to finally live the way God wanted and expected them to live. Conditions were optimal for their being a light to shine through the darkness and let men and women know about God's love. Under Solomon's leadership, the nation lived in peace and prosperity and devoted to God. That is, they did until Solomon started disobeying God's instructions.

Solomon, as the common practice was, often sealed diplomatic ties by marrying foreign princesses. When these women came to live in the Promised Land, they brought their gods with them. The wives insisted on support for their priests and places of worship where they could burn incense and offer sacrifices to their gods. To follow other gods in any sense was to deny what God wanted, and supporting the priests and the wives called for a great deal of money. Solomon himself lived lavishly. His luxurious lifestyle which included fourteen hundred chariots and twelve thousand horses and his many building projects also required a lot of money. Solomon demanded taxes from the people to pay for the pagan temples, their priests, his wives and his extravagant lifestyle. Solomon eventually worshiped his wives' gods, breaking Israel's covenant with God.

God's people in the United Kingdom became frustrated and quarreled among themselves about the heavy tax burden King Solomon placed on them. Their frustration erupted in rebellion when Solomon died. They weren't ready as a group to follow a new leader. In their dissatisfaction, the *United* Kingdom unraveled and came to an end.

Chapter 9

Kingdom Splits, Prophets Warn

The United Kingdom became two independent kingdoms. Ten of the tribes of Israel united to form the Northern Kingdom. This area would also be known as Israel. Two tribes, Judah and Benjamin, clung together in the south. Their space was known as the Southern Kingdom or Judah, and it is where Jerusalem was located.

These two Kingdoms coexisted with both having kings. The kings led for various amounts of time so the controlling powers were continually shifting. Consequently, it was a time of internal warfare and of severe struggle to survive for God's people, whether they resided in the Northern Kingdom or the Southern Kingdom.

Religiously and morally the Northern Kingdom declined. None of their kings pleased the Lord. Often the kings were described as doing evil in the sight of the Lord. The people acted similarly; they were wicked and idolatrous.

The Southern Kingdom had some kings who sought to obey the Lord, but others succumbed to idolatry and wayward living. The worship of idols was a continual temptation for God's people in Judah even though they had the Jerusalem Temple and its priests to assist them in worshiping and serving God.

Around the Northern and Southern Kingdoms, outside the Promised Land, much movement was taking place. Various rulers of powerful nations dreamed of world conquests and sent out armies to conquer rival nations. Syria, Assyria, Babylonia, and Egypt were all involved in these international struggles, and they kept their eyes on the Promised Land.

With these power-seeking nations ever watching, it would have been wise for the kings and the people in the Promised Land to listen to the prophets. Just as both the Northern and Southern Kingdoms had kings, both sides had prophets. The prophets were called by God to be His spokespersons. The prophets openly declared God's will and had being doing so for some time. This period, though, of the Divided Kingdom was one of great prophetic activity. Men like Elijah, Elisha, Jeremiah, Isaiah, Hosea and Amos sought to keep alive true faith and worship. The prophets worked overtime in trying to preserve righteousness and justice. They saw—and predicted—what would happen if God's people persisted in being unfaithful. They warned: "You had better shape up and live the way God wants you to live or you will lose the land."

The people of the Northern Kingdom ignored the warnings of the prophets. Their continual idolatry and rebellion resulted in a weak and corrupt nation. This left them open to attack. When the Assyrians gained power, they conquered the Northern Kingdom around 722-721 B.C. and took many of its residents away as captives. Their vacated land was settled by people groups who had been victims of Assyrian conquests elsewhere.

You would think the Southern Kingdom would have learned from the example of their northern neighbors, but they didn't. Judah also didn't heed the warnings of the prophets. Their disobedience weakened them so they were unable to defend themselves against the Babylonians who had conquered the Assyrians. When the Babylonians defeated God's people in Judah, Jerusalem fell, the Temple was destroyed, and the city walls torn down. This occurred around 587-586 BC.

Many of God's people living in Judah were exiled—taken as captives in Babylon. They no longer were associated with the Promised Land. The Chosen People from both the Northern Kingdom and the Southern Kingdom are now scattered. Other groups now occupy the land God promised His people. Wasn't the land supposed to be theirs? Does this mean God is a promise breaker? And more importantly, what does this mean for God's people becoming a light to shine across the gap of separation? Is this still possible?

Chapter 10

Exile Solidified, Knowledge Gained

Anytime you move to another state or another country it is difficult even if you wanted to make the move. But when you are forced to move to a place radically different from what you've known, it is especially difficult. Exiled in Babylon, God's people lamented, "How can we sing God's song in a foreign land?" (Psalm 137:4 KJV).

At least they weren't slaves. They were colonists so they were free to make choices about how they lived. They could own businesses, sell their products, congregate together and go about their lives. As time went on, many of them made adjustments to living in Babylon, some more than others. There was much to do and to learn in a new land.

Naturally some of God's people gravitated toward others from back home—something people often do when they are strangers in a foreign land. God's people in Babylon began getting together on a regular basis. The Babylonians took note of this and started referring to them as "those people from Judah." Eventually this was shortened to "Jews."

As they met, they shared writings they had brought with them. The writings probably included the Mosaic Law and perhaps the geographical descriptions of where the tribes settled, meaningful psalms and often repeated proverbs. They collected together what writings they had among themselves, read them and studied them.

Because of their history, they were very much aware that things could be lost so they wanted copies of their writings made. They called on scribes to do this. A scribe is anyone who writes. During this time, a professional group of scribes developed. They meticulously and carefully copied documents so they could be exchanged, read, reread and studied.

As God's people assembled together, read and shared their writings, they learned God could be experienced in a foreign land. Back in Judah, God's people had clung to the idea that God could only be experienced in Jerusalem at the Temple. In exile, they found out that God was present and could be worshiped in other places.

As they met together, fellowshipping and discussing their collected writings, it occurred to them that they could do this on a regular basis. Here's where the *concept* of a synagogue (a gathering together, an assembly) was born! They carried this idea with them when they returned home, and God's people did get to return.

God remembered His land promise and opened the way for God's people to go back to Judah. This move probably doesn't surprise you, but the way it happened might. The Babylonians were defeated by the Persians. Their leader, Cyrus, was not a believer in the God of Abraham, Isaac and Jacob, but he believed a people served best when they could be in their own area so he allowed God's people to return to Judah. They wouldn't be in charge of themselves; the Persians would still be in control, but they could go home if they wanted to. Not everyone chose to return.

God's people had been in exile seventy years. Captives had died, children had been born, and memories had dimmed so not everyone was interested in returning to Judah. A remnant, though, was. They went home with a new name, a new concept, collected writings, and more importantly, they went home believing the God of Abraham, Isaac and Jacob was the one true God. What the prophets had predicted came true which led God's people to conclude that God was indeed who He said He was. He was the one true God! This realization was so profound that it wiped out the sin of idolatry for the Chosen People once and for all. From now on, they would be a people of one God!

Chapter 11

Remnant Return, Rebuilding Needed

Things are never the same when you go back home after being away for years. The place is never quite like what you remember. Judah, the former Southern Kingdom, wasn't for the people who had once lived there or for those born in captivity who had heard stories about "back home."

God's people were heartbroken at what they saw when they arrived back in Judah. Jerusalem was in ruins. The Temple was gone. The city walls leveled. And while they were back in "their land," the land wasn't actually theirs. The Persians were still in control, and they appointed governors to represent them locally. Each governor in Judah was assisted by the Jewish high priest (someone from the tribe of Levi, specifically a descendant of Aaron, Moses' brother, as directed in the law given during the Exodus).

Still it was good to be back in the Promised Land. God's people went about rebuilding their city, the walls, and the Temple. They encountered challenge after challenge.

With the help of Ezra, a scribe and priest, and Nehemiah, a Persian-appointed governor, God's people persevered. What resulted, though, didn't match what their ancestors had known, and this discouraged them. They longed for times like David's and Solomon's early years when they weren't under the control or domination of another nation, when they had wealth and power, and when the Temple was magnificent. The rebuilt Temple was smaller and less grand than Solomon's Temple. When, they wondered, was God going to revive the glory days of David and Solomon? Throughout their history there had been hints that someone was going to appear, someone who would change everything. Who was this person? When was he going to come? And how would they recognize him?

In addition to the physical rebuilding of the Temple, the walls and the city, God's people set about rebuilding their faith. As long as they recognized the supremacy of Persia and observed Persian laws, they were free to exercise their faith, and they did, more intentionally than ever before. They realized that the Exile came about because of their failure to live according to God's instructions. Determined that such a failure would not happen again, "they elevated the Word of God to new heights of importance and strictly applied the principles of the law to everyday life."[1]

- God's people studied the books of the law. They met together in groups as they started doing while captive in Babylon. As time passed, these gatherings became associated with buildings known as synagogues. Synagogues sprung up in Jerusalem and eventually wherever Jews lived, such as those who had been scattered during the Assyrian and Babylonian captivities.
- They dutifully and consistently performed the rite of circumcision, something they were supposed to have done from the time of Abraham, but didn't always practice.
- They emphasized prayer, fasting, alms-giving, Sabbath keeping, and food regulations—things delineated in the Mosaic Law.

This is not to say that God's people found it easy to keep so many laws. Prophets such as Haggai, Zechariah and Malachi had to prod them and preach to them about their lapses. But just like they did in rebuilding the city, the Temple, and the walls, God's people persevered. They did so well that an air of exclusivity developed among God's people. As they took what they had learned in Exile and what they now devoted themselves to, they concluded they were indeed God's Chosen People. This conclusion interfered with God's people drawing men and women to God. What's God, the Initiator, going to do about this? How's He going to see to it that all people may experience His love and have a relationship with Him?

The Time In Between

When we position ourselves to take a panoramic view of a landscape, we notice landmarks, things that stand out to us. Sometimes, though, as we gaze, we see empty spaces–places where the terrain changes. No trees are growing, shrubs have disappeared, and the land is flat instead of hilly. And then it picks up again with vegetation and hills reappearing. When we take a panoramic view of the Bible, something similar takes place. Between the history, the stories, the prayers, the sayings of the Old and New Testaments is an empty space. This space covers 400 years. The Bible doesn't tell us what happened during that time which is why they are often called the silent years.

Significant things happened during that time, though, and when I learned what transpired, I was better able to understand how the events of the New Testament unfolded. This knowledge helped me read, study and teach the Bible, which is why I want to share it with you.

The information for what happened between the Testaments comes from the apocryphal books (which some Bibles include), the writings of Josephus (a Jewish historian), the Dead Sea scrolls and secular history. Gaining a basic knowledge of what happened between the testaments cleared up a lot of mysteries for me and answered a lot of questions I had about the differences between the Old and New Testament. I invite you to "stand with me" and let's look together at the time between the testaments. Perhaps you'll find, as I did, that the silent years aren't so silent after all.

Chapter 12
Talk Expanded, Lifestyle Challenged

When the Old Testament closes, the Persians are in charge. Under various Persian leaders, they maintain control until Alexander the Great, a Greek leader, started making conquests. By now, the Promised Land, formerly Canaan, is now called Palestine. It was one of the areas Alexander conquered. Nothing changed as far as the Jews being able to practice their faith. Alexander had a good relationship with them and allowed them to continue to be devoted to their rules and rituals, although he probably preferred they become more Greek-like. He was devoted to Hellenism.

Hellenism is a label given to the Greek way of life. Alexander was a passionate disciple of Hellenism. He believed that he was obligated to spread Greek culture wherever he went, including the language. The Greek language was beautiful, refined, and precise, and it "caught on." Most people began speaking Greek. They didn't give up their own languages. They added Greek as a second language and used it in business and in government dealings.

While Alexander was passionate about Greek culture, he didn't try to force it on his subjects. Even though the Jews were not in charge of themselves, they were free to be God's representatives, and the Greek language provided them an important tool for doing this. A language barrier wouldn't prevent Jews from being a light to others, but something else Greek-related might interfere.

Other aspects of Hellenism challenged the lifestyle of God's people. To Greeks, life was good and meant to be enjoyed. Pleasure of all kinds was not only legitimate but desirable. Life should be enjoyed not in the future but now.

Greeks stressed health, games, sports and activities. Gyms and stadiums were built; participants competed in the nude.

They greatly appreciated music, theater, literature and the arts, attending these events and participating in them.

Great libraries were built. Philosophical discussions held, and mental gymnastics encouraged.

The Greeks stressed proper styles with some of them being gaudy and outrageous,

The passion of the Greeks about their way of life was contagious. People in the places they conquered, including some Jews, adopted their ways. Other Jews, though, bristled at the thought of being Hellenists. To them, giving attention to proper style and personal appearance was frivolous and wicked. To participate in sports in the nude was outrageous!

This difference in responses to Hellenism caused a hairline crack to develop within the Jewish community. Some argued that you could be a Hellenist and still be a good Jew while others insisted you couldn't. Fortunately, at this time, no one was forcing Jews to accept Hellenism.

Alexander died unexpectedly at age 33. No plan was in place for a successor; therefore, the territory he conquered was divided among four of his generals. Palestine, which included Judea (formerly Judah) and Jerusalem, happened to be sandwiched between two of the generals.

- General Ptolemy was given the southern or Egyptian section which was south of Palestine.
- Another general, Seleucus, was given Syria which lay north of Palestine.

Both Ptolemy and Seleucus and their respective descendants coveted Palestine. Consequently, many battles were fought between the Egyptian Ptolemies and the Syrian Seleucids. Too many to count! Eventually, the Syrians gained firm control of Palestine.

All during this time, Jews weren't pressed to adopt Hellenism. This changed under the leadership of the Syrian ruler, Antiochus Epiphanes. Obsessed with Hellenism, he was determined to force his subjects into cultural and religious unity. He insisted everyone practice Hellenism and worship Greek deities. He made observing the Sabbath, performing the rite of circumcision, and possessing sacred writings punishable by death. He aimed to destroy the worship of the God of Abraham, Isaac, and Jacob. Would he succeed?

Chapter 13
Conformity Demanded, Courage Responded

Antiochus Epiphanes' determination to force his subjects into cultural and religious unity fueled the anger of the Jews. Unhappy relations developed between them. They disliked him so much that when they heard he was killed while away from Palestine on a campaign in Egypt, the Jews proceeded at once to celebrate. They learned later that the report was false.

When Antiochus returned to Jerusalem and heard about the celebration, he wreaked his vengeance on the city and plundered the Temple. Naturally, this increased the enmity between Antiochus and the Jews.

Antiochus persuaded some Hellenistic Jews to join his forces in his attempt to make all Jews conform. Many Jews, though, resisted and were imprisoned. Forty thousand were slaughtered and an equal number were sold as slaves. Antiochus sent emissaries to the synagogues where God's people assembled on the Sabbath. They massacred thousands of men, women and children.

To further show his contempt for the faith of the Jews, Antiochus sacrificed a pig on the altar in the Temple. He cooked the meat and then poured the broth over all the building. He had an altar to the Greek god Zeus erected in the Temple area. He was determined to destroy the worship of the God of Abraham, Isaac and Jacob.

This defilement of the Jews' sacred place ignited a revolt. At first their resistance to Antiochus' actions was passive, but later their resistance became a burning flame.

The person who struck the match that lit the flame was an old Jewish priest named Mattathias. He and his five sons lived in Modein, a little town west of Jerusalem. His family is sometimes called Asmonaeans or Hasmonaeans, a label derived from one of their ancestors. They are more frequently called Maccabeans which may have been a nickname meaning "hammerers."

When testing the loyalty of the people, Antiochus sent a representative to Modein where he built an altar to Zeus. He commanded Mattathias and his sons to offer sacrifices to this pagan god. He even promised them a large reward if they would do it. The Maccabeans refused. A young Jewish man in the group stepped forward to obey the order. To him, it was no big deal. His act angered Mattathias, and without considering the consequences, he rushed forward and killed the young man. He then killed Antiochus' agent. Realizing he would now be a wanted man, Mattathias made an appeal to Jews who felt the same way to rebel. He and his five sons, together with other zealous Jews, declared war on Antiochus. They fled to the hills where other Jews joined them. A courageous army was formed and gorilla warfare ensued.

Leading a revolt was too strenuous for Mattathias. He turned the leadership over to Judas, one of his sons. Under Judas' leadership, the rebelling Jews won religious freedom for themselves even though they were outnumbered. They were now free to worship God without molestation or harassment.

Under the guidance of another of Mattathias' sons, Simon, the Jews fought for and won political freedom. They were now in charge of themselves. All payment of taxes to Syria ceased. As Simon assumed civil leadership, he also assumed the role of Jewish high priest. His reign was one of great prosperity, and they were free of any outside dominance. A new era of independence was underway. The Jews were in the land God promised them, they were in charge of themselves, they were prospering, and they could freely follow God's instructions for living. They even had a language in common with other people groups. The time was ripe for them to fully shine as a light in the darkness. Perhaps they would have if it weren't for that hairline crack. It started widening. Do you remember what that crack was?

Chapter 14
Freedom Gained, Freedom Lost

The hairline crack first appeared when Jews were confronted with Hellenism. Some felt you could be a Hellenist and be a good Jew; others felt you couldn't. After Simon Maccabeus gained political freedom, something happened that widened the crack. The civil ruler and the high priest became one and the same. This brought new power—and to some, a disturbing power—to the office of high priest, a religious role.

The more pious Jews—the ones who thought you couldn't be a Hellenist *and* be a good Jew—reacted against the secularization of the priesthood. Others, though, didn't see it as a problem. They were more interested in political control than being religiously observant. As the gap widened, two religious parties developed.

The Pharisees. They were interested in religious freedom, keeping the priesthood a spiritual role, rigidly following both the written law given to Moses and the oral laws that were developing. Since the Mosaic Law was supposed to cover every detail of life, specific interpretations were continually added. These interpretations weren't written down. They were passed on orally and meticulously followed by the Pharisees.

The Sadducees. Their interest was maintaining political control so the secularization of the priesthood didn't bother them. Neither were they concerned about Jews adopting aspects of Hellenism. They were loyal to the written law, the law God had given the people through Moses.

This is not to say that every Jew was a member of one group or the other. They weren't, but it is to say that the groups were powerful, affecting those in leadership and thereby influencing the direction of the nation. After Simon's death, leadership continued under Macabbean descendants. The allegiance of those in charge varied. Sometimes a leader was pro Sadducee, and other times the leader was devoted to Pharisaical ideals. Fighting and wrangling prevailed. The antagonism between these two parties became so severe it weakened the country. They were so caught up in internal strife that they were unaware of a growing menace rising up around them. The Roman Empire was expanding! As the Romans annexed new territories, they had their eyes on Palestine.

In 63 BC, the Romans took possession of Palestine which included Judea, and Jewish independence came to an end. God's people were back in a subservient position. For everyday living, this wasn't as restrictive as it sounds. The Romans brought peace and stability to the area. They improved travel by building roads and clearing waterways of piracy. As long as their subjects paid taxes and provided soldiers for maintaining peace, people's everyday lives didn't change that much.

If a province showed loyalty to the Roman Empire, its citizens were allowed to continue their religious practices. They could keep their local customs, laws, money system, and sometimes their local rulers. As power struggles for leadership took place in Judea, the Romans stepped in. They appointed the local leaders such as procurators, tetrarchs and governors. The Jewish High Priest served under an appointed leader in Judea.

While their lives didn't change drastically under Roman control, the Jews didn't like being dominated by them. A spirit of unrest and dissatisfaction developed among God's people. They longed for someone to help them regain political control. But as they looked back at their history, they realized this was never going to happen by their own efforts. If they were to ascend to their rightful place of leadership, God would have to send someone, an Anointed One, a Messiah, a prophet like Moses, or a Son of David to deliver them. He would defeat the Romans and usher them into their rightful place of authority. Who would be the person to lead the Jews to freedom and their rightful place? Who would be their deliverer? And when, oh when, would he come?

Chapter 15

Prophets Quiet, Rules Prevail

Have you noticed there's been no mention of prophets speaking during this time between the testaments? There weren't any on the scene; at least, none that we know of. In fact some people call the time between the testaments the "silent years" because there's no record of prophets being used to declare God's will. It could be, though, that some prophets did speak, but God's people weren't paying attention. Their focus wasn't on hearing; it was on the law.

Instead of leaning on the prophets for motivation and direction, God's people devoted themselves to the law. "The law was considered to be absolute, complete, and infallible . . . This outlook left no place for the individual experience or viewpoint. No one was free to speak on religious matters in Israel unless he spoke on how to keep or magnify the law."[2]

This dedication to the law sounds like a really good thing. But in reality, dedication to the law was mixed. It was good in that it showed God's people learned from their Exile experience. They didn't want a repeat experience so they earnestly and sincerely tried to live the way God wanted them to live. Plus the law unified them as a people. Wherever they were located, whether it was in Jerusalem, Babylon, Egypt or Syria, their identity as Jews was molded by the law. This set them apart distinctively as the worshipers of One God–the God of Abraham, Isaac, and Jacob.

Over time, though, a problem developed. This is where the "not so good" part comes in! Religion for many Jews became "largely a matter of engaging in detailed rituals and obeying fixed rules of conduct."[3] God's people were so earnest in keeping the written law of Moses, they began making specific interpretations of its broad principles. For example, the Mosaic Law said "thou shalt not do any work" on the "Sabbath" (Exodus 20:10 KJV). The scribes, who were interpreters of the law, reasoned, If we are to keep this commandment, we need to know what activities constitute work and what does not. Obviously, threshing grain and lifting burdens were work and therefore prohibited, but what about plucking out a gray hair? Or if a wad of cotton worn in one's ear happened to fall out, would it constitute lifting a burden if you picked it up? You get the picture.

The scribes sorted out numerous questions like these and created specific rules to follow. Their rules weren't written down so the Mosaic Law wasn't changed. Their interpretations were passed on by word of mouth and as a group became known as the Oral Law. Over time, the number of oral rules grew larger and larger.

Those who attempted to obey the oral laws saw their efforts as pleasing God. They lost sight of—or perhaps they never fully understood—the law was given to assist them in being God's representatives and drawing others to Him. The many detailed oral laws had the opposite effect.

The numerous rules discouraged people from coming to God. Their attitude was "I never could keep all those rules. It would be impossible so I might as well not even try." Instead, they continued on in darkness, living meaningless lives. Morals were low, and immorality was openly displayed. Pessimism and fatalism prevailed. They needed a light to shine through the darkness so they could know God and experience Him.

What's God, the Initiator, going to do about this dilemma? How's He going to penetrate their hearts and thinking? Will He call a prophet to preach to them? Publish a scroll? Speak in an audible voice? Hang an unusual star in the sky? Send a Super Hero? What's it going to take so people can see Him?

The New Testament

Chapter 16

Light Arrives, People Unaware

For God so loved the world that He sent a part of Himself—He sent a baby. His Son, Jesus, was born in Bethlehem, a little town near Jerusalem. Only a few people recognized the significance of what was taking place. Shepherds on a hillside, alerted by angels who said a Savior was born, rushed to Bethlehem to see Him. Wisemen from another country came later to see baby Jesus. They called Him "king of the Jews." Herod, the Roman-appointed ruler over Palestine, worried that this baby "king" might be the Messiah, the One the Jewish people were looking for. An old couple at the Temple in Jerusalem saw Him as being a light to the Gentiles and as bringing glory to God's people. The light had arrived! It would take awhile, though, for others to recognize Him as Savior, King, and Messiah.

Jesus grew up in Nazareth in Galilee, an area of Palestine. As a young adult, He worked as a carpenter until He was around thirty years old. At that time, He left home and began teaching, preaching, healing, exorcizing demons, and performing miracles throughout Palestine.

At first, people paid little attention to Him, but as stories of His healings and things He said spread, people flocked to see Him and to hear Him. They marveled at His compassionate power and the way He spoke with authority.

Jesus talked a lot about God as if He were trying to show people what God was really like and what God desired for them. The people heard how God wanted all people to relate to Him and to care for each other. As Jesus talked about God, some wondered, *Could He be sent from God?*

Some listeners were so attracted to Jesus that they left their work and families to travel with Him. They wanted to learn from Him and be associated with Him; they became His disciples.

Jesus' popularity soared when He taught and healed in the heavily populated area of Galilee. With so many people responding to His message and with His ability to perform miracles, many speculated, *Could he be the Messiah, the Anointed One we've been looking for?*

His talk about God and the crowds surrounding Jesus aroused the interest of the Pharisees and scribes. Because of their devotion to the oral laws, they were disturbed by some of the things Jesus said and did. He challenged some of their rules and rituals! He acted contrary to what they perceived as right. They started showing up in places where He was preaching and teaching. They weren't interested in learning from Him and heeding His messages. Rather they hoped to discredit Him. As they listened to Jesus, they concluded, *This man must not be allowed to continue!* They were especially irked regarding Jesus' use—or rather abuse as they saw it—of the Sabbath. Once after Jesus had plucked grain and healed a man on the Sabbath (both rule-breaking acts), they discussed "how they might destroy him" (Mark 3:6c KJV).

The Sadducees were slower to take an interest in Him. They didn't care that Jesus was breaking rules. They became interested in Him when He started attracting large crowds. This man had power! If He were the Messiah, as some people were speculating, this made Jesus a political threat. Even though the Romans were in charge, the Jews still mostly governed themselves. The Sadducees played a large part in maintaining control and settling disputes; they didn't want to lose that power so they joined in the opposition. Jesus must be stopped. They never realized that God had taken on human form and flesh and was dwelling among them (see John 1:14). The light was present but they were unaware. What would it take for them—and for us—to see the light?

Chapter 17
Darkness Hovers, Light Shines

Those opposed to Jesus learned that confronting Him, ridiculing Him and trying to trick Him didn't discourage Him. Jesus kept right on speaking, ministering and gaining followers. Consequently, His opponents became even more determined. Killing Him, they decided, was the obvious solution, but that would get *them* into trouble! Wanting to avoid being arrested, Jesus' enemies conspired to legally bring about Jesus' death, and they convinced others to help them.

A crowd armed with swords and clubs arrested Jesus and brought Him before the court of the Jews so they could find Him guilty of something punishable by death. Since Jesus hadn't done anything wrong, false accusations were made. The court found Jesus guilty of blasphemy, a crime that called for the death penalty.

Still more was needed, though, if God's people were to legally bring about Jesus' death. While Jews ruled themselves in many ways, the Romans, the government in charge, reserved the right to issue the death penalty. This meant the Jews would have to let Pilate, the Roman-appointed leader of Judea, decide what to do with Jesus.

Members of the Jewish court knew that Pilate would not take seriously the charge of blasphemy, a religious crime, so they made up charges that he would consider. They said that Jesus perverted the nation, refused to pay taxes and was going to set himself up as King. As Pilate listened to the charges, he realized Jesus was innocent. Nevertheless, to please the Jews with whom he didn't have a good relationship, he sentenced Jesus to die on a cross.

Crucifixion was an intensely painful way to execute a person. The victims died a slow, agonizing death while onlookers watched. In the horror of the moment, darkness covered the earth. Even Jesus felt the sting of the darkness. From the cross, he cried out, "My God, my God, why hast thou forsaken me?"

But God, the Creator, the Initiator, did not forget Jesus nor His desire for people to know Him. Through Jesus' death on the cross, God was showing men and women and boys and girls that there is no limit to His love. On that awful day when darkness hovered, He was saying, "I love you so much that I'm willing to let my own Son die on a cross to show you." We wouldn't know this, though, if it wasn't for what happened next.

Jesus did not stay dead! He came back to life! He appeared to His followers which made them realize Jesus was truly sent from God. If He had died and stayed dead, He would have been just another good man dying an undeserved death. Many good men have died this way throughout history, but Jesus' resurrection proved His deity. It proved He was sent from God! He was God's message of love to the world! The light had come! It cost Jesus' His life for us to know this, for us to know how much God loves us!

The disciples wondered at various times through out Jesus' ministry about who He was. They had pinned their hopes on Him as they caught glimmers of who He was. When Jesus' died, they lost hope. As two disciples said, they "had hoped that he would be the one who was going to set Israel free!" (Luke 24:21 TEV). But as Jesus appeared to the disciples numerous times in His resurrection body, hope returned. This man they had followed, who they had seen perform miracles and cast out demons, and who they had heard preach and teach was sent from God. In fact, He was God! The light had come and had overcame the darkness making it possible for men, women, boys and girls to realize God loves them and wants to have a relationship with them. To see the cross is to see the light.

Chapter 18

Power Comes, Light Spreads

While the disciples were convinced Jesus was alive, there might have been some hesitancy on their part to talk about it. People might respond in disbelief. *You say Jesus died and came back to life?! You say He is God?* Or they might hold back because they knew how Jesus was treated. He was ridiculed, mocked, mistreated, whipped and ultimately put to death. They weren't eager to experience similar treatment, but if they didn't witness, how were people going to see the light? They needed some help if they were to be witnesses of His resurrection "in Jerusalem, in all of Judea and Samaria, and to the ends of the earth" (Acts 1:8 TEV) as Jesus said they would be. That "something more" was the Holy Spirit.

In Jerusalem during the Jewish festival of Pentecost, Jesus' Spirit descended and empowered His followers to boldly talk about Him, and they did! Jesus' followers told people about their leader who showed them what God was like, who died and who did not stay dead. As some witnesses moved out beyond Jerusalem, the witnesses were ridiculed or persecuted, but they persevered. They had seen the light, witnessed the resurrection and possessed the power of His Spirit.

They were also aware that they continued to experience Jesus—as if He were right there with them. Before His death, Jesus was limited by time and space. To interact with Him, you had to actually be in His physical presence. Now, through the power of the Holy Spirit, Jesus was no longer bound. Wherever believers were, they could know and experience Jesus.

Those who believed in Jesus met in groups to talk about Jesus, to pray, to worship and to listen to the instruction of those who had known Him in the flesh. The groups formed churches, gathering together in much the same way Jews gathered in synagogues.

As the number of churches grew, the Jews who had been disturbed by Jesus' teachings—those who had brought about His death—were likewise disturbed by this growing movement. They saw this development as yet another threat to their faith. One very conscientious Jew named Paul, a Pharisee, was especially disturbed. As a zealous defender of his faith, he determined to stamp out the church. In the process, Paul saw the light! He became a believer in Jesus.

Paul was convinced that Jesus was sent by God. He believed that if you accepted Jesus as being God's Son, the gulf of separation between humans and God could be bridged. He began talking about Jesus and trying to persuade other Jews to accept Him.

He traveled throughout the Roman Empire telling the story of Jesus. He traveled on those roads the Romans had built to connect various areas of the Empire. He sailed the Mediterranean Sea which the Romans had made safer for travel.

Those synagogues that developed following the Exile provided ready platforms for Paul to speak. They were located in places where Jews lived. Rabbis and Pharisees like Paul were welcomed to speak during the synagogue service, and Paul took advantage of this platform.

In most places, Paul's message about Jesus was warmly received by some of the Jews. When this happened, others responded with jealousy and anger. Those involved in the backlash mistreated Paul, and often ran him out of town. To this treatment, Paul responded, "I will take my message to the Gentiles," and he did, spreading the light wherever he went.

This meant non-Jews as well as Jews would be able to learn that God loved them and wanted a relationship with them. Men and women everywhere could hear the story of Jesus, and realize Jesus was—and is—the light. If they embraced the light, they could experience His love and guidance. They would be God's people.

Chapter 19

Questions Asked, Answers Given

Years ago, I heard someone say, "All that happened before Jesus was anticipatory; what happened afterwards was explanatory." What needed explaining? If you believed Jesus was God's Son who died on the cross so you would feel His love and not be estranged from God simple enough to understand? In one sense, it was. Believing in God, being put right with Him, is not complicated. But in another sense, believers needed help in applying their faith. They had questions that needed answering.

(1) *What does believing in Jesus mean for everyday living*? What did it mean for the casual Jew who saw the light? To those Jews earnest about keeping the oral laws? Should they continue or discontinue living by rules and regulations? What did living for Jesus mean to Gentiles without previous exposure to godly principles such as the Ten Commandments? To Gentiles living in completely pagan areas? If a person really believed that the God of the Universe sent His Son to die on a cross, what difference is this going to make—or should make—in an individual's life? New believers needed instructions to help them understand how faith and action are related.

(2) *How do believers live and worship together when they come from a variety of backgrounds*? People were coming to faith from various circumstances and areas throughout the Roman Empire, and they brought their backgrounds with them. People in Jerusalem didn't think like or live like the people in Corinth, in Athens or in Antioch, places where Paul and others taught and preached. How could these people work and fellowship together when their eating habits differed? When some practiced circumcision and others didn't? Some Jews thought Gentiles ought to be circumcised to be put right with God? The rite had been important to them. Why shouldn't Gentiles be required to do what they were required to do to please God? Gentiles found it hard to give up pagan ideas and practices that were important to them. People needed guidance if they were to work, worship and fellowship together in churches.

(3) *Who are we to believe*? It was hard for believers to ignore their backgrounds, their ideas and their practices. The result in some areas was the rising up of teachers

who corrupted the Christian message. A teacher might have held to a religious concept from his past, or he might have blended Christian truth with Greek philosophies, pagan gods or Roman practices. Whatever the cause, errors needed to be identified and refuted. Here's where the witness of Jesus' apostles was so important. The Spirit helped the apostles recall what they had seen Him do and heard Him say. They helped the churches counter false teachers and line up the truth with Jesus, His nature, what He taught, and how He lived.

These are some of the questions that men and women grappled with as they accepted the truth of what Paul, the apostles and others preached about Jesus. When they could, these men answered these questions face to face. When they were ministering in particular locations, they had discussions, led people to conclusions and helped them develop Christian principles. But when the leaders moved on, new problems occurred and new questions were sometimes raised. Letters were written and sermons circulated to answer questions, to resolve problems, to give instruction and to encourage believers.

Paul was the most prolific of the letter writers. He wrote 13 letters to churches and to individuals. Other explainers were James, John, Jude, Peter and one whose name we do not know (the writer of Hebrews). Questions were asked and answers were given. Through it all, the light shined and will continue to shine—some say even brighter—in the days to come.

Chapter 20
Troubles Threaten, Light Endures

As the number of believers grew and developed, friction developed between Christ followers and Jews. Since the Exile, the Jews had made the law front and center of their lives. They believed this put them right with God. Christians said "Believe on the Lord Jesus Christ, and thou shalt be saved" (Acts 16:31 KJV). This teaching was unacceptable to many Jews plus it was hard for some of them to accept the idea that God's light was for Gentiles as well as for them. As a result, they interfered with the work of Christians and at times persecuted them.

The Roman government didn't pay much attention to this friction between the two. They thought Christians were a sect of Judaism so they paid little attention to local dynamics between them. Eventually, though, it became clear that a separate faith was developing—Christianity. This emerging group fell under Rome's ban on new superstitions so they kept an eye on Christians. The Roman government was vigilant in making sure they had loyal subjects and maintained a peaceful and stable environment.

The distrust of Christians accelerated when Nero was emperor of the Roman Empire. A great fire had destroyed almost one-fourth of the city of Rome. Nero blamed Christians for starting the fire, igniting hatred against Christians among the population.

Conditions got even worse for Christians when Domitian became emperor. Domitian demanded that he be worshiped once a year. This involved bowing before an image of him, offering a pinch of incense, and saying "Caesar is Lord." The rest of the year, participants were free to worship whatever god or gods they chose to serve. If anyone refused to honor Caesar in this way, he was labeled a political rebel. He could be imprisoned, have his property seized, exiled (as the apostle John was to the island of Patmos), or be killed.

Even in light of all those possible consequences, Christians refused to worship Caesar. To them, only Jesus could be called "Lord." They could not bring themselves to say, "Caesar is Lord." Consequently, they were harassed, persecuted and sometimes killed.

With this kind of treatment, you would think Christians would just give up, that the light shining in their hearts would quit glowing. But it didn't. If anything, it shined even brighter. As William Coble once noted, "Men find the glory of their faith and of the presence of God, not in peace, prosperity, and ease, but in struggle, danger, and daring."[4] This didn't mean that Christians didn't need guidance and encouragement during difficult times because they did.

Christians needed counsel concerning the choices they had to make: How do you follow Christ when your life is in danger? What should be the Christian's response to harassment and persecution?

They needed reassurance that evil would not win, that the light would not be snuffed out by the opposition. They needed to have their hope fanned and be encouraged to remain true to following Jesus which is what God-inspired writers did.

Letters such as Hebrews, 1 Peter, and John's Revelation were written and circulated. These books acknowledged the choices which Christians have to make during difficult times and the results of their choices. They provided guidance on how to live and to endure in the face of suffering, reassuring them—and reassuring us today—that the light is strong. It has and will endure. Nothing "can separate us from the love of Christ. . . nothing in all creation . . . will ever be able to separate us from the love of God which is ours through Christ Jesus" (Romans 8: 35, 38, 39 TEV). That's because the God who said, "Let light shine out of darkness," has "made his light shine in our hearts" (2 Corinthians 4:6 NIV). We have seen the light. That's why we can know God and experience His love.

Selected Bibliography

Benware, Paul N. *Survey of the New Testament*. Chicago, Illinois: Moody Publishers, 2003.

Coble, William. *Messages from First-century Christians*. Nashville, Tennessee: Convention Press, 1971.

Cresson, Bruce. "The Impact of the Exile on Israel," *Biblical Illustrator*, Spring 1999, pages 70, 71, 72 and 73.

Hester, H. I. *The Heart of the New Testament*. Liberty, Missouri: The William Jewel Press, 1950.

Hester, H. I. *The Heart of Hebrew History*. Liberty, Missouri: The William Jewel Press, 1949.

House, Paul. *Old Testament Survey*. Nashville, Tennessee: Broadman Press, 1992.

Wayne Grudem, C. John Collins, and Thomas R. Schreiner (editors). *Understanding the Big Picture of the Bible*. Wheaton, Illinois: Crossway, 2012.

Pfeiffer, Charles F. *Between the Testaments*. Grand Rapids, Michigan: Baker Book House, 1959.

Acknowledgements

I appreciate the help and encouragement I received from these people.

My husband, Bob.

My sons: Ben, Jim and Joel.

My friend and co-laborer for Christ, Kristi Neace.

My sister, Judy Mills.

My friend, Jan Turner.

Graphic designer, Betty Manhart, and

Fellow writer, Elaine Colvin.

The writing and printing of a panoramic view of the Bible wouldn't have been possible without their help, and I say "thank you" to each one of them. I am blessed by having them in my life.

Availability to Speak

As I mentioned in the introduction, I give the overview of the Bible in oral presentations. I would welcome the opportunity to share it with your church or group because I love to tell the story. I can provide learning exercises and interactive activities to go along with the "telling" to help participants get a grip on the Bible's content and the inter-biblical period. If your church, group or organization could use a better understanding of the Bible or a refresher course, I would be glad to help. You may contact me through my website **BrendaPoinsett.com**.

---

[1] Paul N. Benware, *Survey of the New Testament* (Chicago: Moody Publishers, 2003), page 19.
[2] Coble, *Messages from First-century Christians* (Nashville, Tennessee: Convention Press, 1971), page 179.
[3] *Ibid.*
[4] *Ibid.*, page 7.

Made in the USA
Coppell, TX
13 January 2022